PESTER POWER GO GREEN!

Catherine Chambers

Published 2009 by
A & C Black Publishers Ltd.
36 Soho Square, London, W1D 3QY
www.acblack.com

ISBN   HB 978-1-4081-0849-9
       PB 978-1-4081-1292-2

Series consultant: Gill Matthews

This book is produced using paper that is made from wood grown in managed, sustainable forests. It is natural, renewable and recyclable. The logging and manufacturing processes conform to the environmental regulations of the country of origin.

Produced for A & C Black by Calcium.
Printed and bound in China by C&C Offset Printing Co.

All the internet addresses given in this book were correct at the time of going to press. The author and publishers regret any inconvenience caused if addresses have changed or sites have ceased to exist, but can accept no responsibility for any such changes.

Acknowledgements
The publishers would like to thank the following for their kind permission to reproduce their photographs:
Cover: Shutterstock: Melissa Schalke top, Kyle Smith bottom.
Pages: Dreamstime: Mika Specta 17, Mark Yuill 12; Istockphoto: Ian Hamilton 13, David Parsons 14; Shutterstock: Mark Atkins 11, Hagit Berkovich 7, Archana Bhartia 15, Sebastien Burel 6, Victor Burnside 21t, Terrance Emerson 10, Eray Haciosmanoglu 16, Cheryl Hill 4, Palis Michael 5, Norman Pogson 21b, Jose AS Reyes 9b, Christina Richards 20, Mark William Richardson 18, Otmar Smit 9t.

CONTENTS

WHY SHOULD WE CARE?

Our precious planet is changing fast. The weather is wilder and natural landscapes are disappearing. It is also getting harder to grow enough food to feed everyone.

What's the problem?

Earth has heated up in the last 200 years. This is because we've burned a lot of **fossil fuels**, such as coal and oil. This releases harmful gases into the air.

Think about how you would feel if this mountain lost its snow, or the trees lost their leaves and died. Do you want to do something to help our planet now?

A power station with billowing fumes.

What does it mean?

The seas around the British Isles have risen by 10 cm (4 in) in the last 100 years, and they are still rising. Wild birds and butterflies are disappearing because they don't have food at the right time of year.

What can we do?

We can learn more about how the planet works. We can learn about our **carbon footprint**. That's a measure of the amount of energy we use.

The United Nations Environment Programme (UNEP) can help us keep in touch.

What do you know about our planet?

WATER WORRIES

We need to worry about water. In some parts of the world there isn't enough. In other parts of the world there is just too much.

Wild weather

Weather patterns are changing. In some places, dry periods are lasting much longer. This causes drought. In other places, rainfall has become much heavier. That leads to flooding. Drought and floods have forced 25 million people across Africa and Asia to move.

What a waste

In England and Wales broken water pipes leak huge amounts of water. A dripping tap wastes 90 litres (20 gallons) of water a week. Water is precious, so why are we wasting it?

Watering holes, such as this one, dry up during a drought. With no water to drink, whole herds of **livestock** may die.

Action around the world

It is difficult for many people in developing countries to find safe drinking water. WaterAid is a charity that helps people with water needs. You can found out more on their website: www.wateraid.org.uk

WATCH THAT WATER!

Can you guess how much water you use at home? One day, make a note each time you have a drink, turn on a tap and flush the toilet. Think about ways of reducing and **recycling** the water you use. Here are some ideas to get you started:

* Turn the tap off when you clean your teeth.

* Water plants with washing-up water.

* Take a shower instead of a bath.

Aid charities provide many people in Africa with clean drinking water.

7

FRAGILE FORESTS

Hedgerows, forests, and woodlands are being destroyed all over the world. Trees are cut down for firewood and **timber**. They are also cut down to clear the land for farming.

WHY SHOULD WE SAVE TREES?

* Forests are the lungs of the world. They produce **oxygen** that we breathe.

* The world's forests hold at least 60 per cent of all animal and plant **species**.

* They are the biggest **habitats** for **bacteria**, **fungi** and **mosses** that break down plant matter.

* Many forest plants give us important medicines, and there are many more waiting to be discovered.

* Roots hold the soil together. Without them, there are dangerous mudslides when it rains.

* Leaves from forest trees soak up harmful carbon gases. So forests help stop wild weather.

Action around the world

Many people in the developing world cook on stoves that run on **charcoal** or solar power. Many countries are protecting their forests and planting trees to make new forests.

Solar panels are used to heat water in the home.

What can we do?

Take a large piece of recycled paper. Write down a charter for trees like the one on page 8. You could hang it up at home or at school to show people how important trees are.

Timber is used for making furniture and paper.

FARMING FOREVER

Some types of farming are damaging the planet. We need to think about how we are going to carry on producing food in the future.

What's the problem?

Many soaps, **cosmetics**, and even toothpastes are made from palm oil. Some farmers clear forests to grow palm trees. Other farmers burn grasslands to sow **cereals** to make **biofuels**. Biofuels are cleaner than petrol and oil. But clearing wild areas is damaging the planet.

This field of crops is being harvested. It will all be used for biofuels.

Action around the world

We need to eat more locally grown food. This food is fresher and less fuel is used to transport it. In Europe, the Slow Food Movement is supporting locally grown food. They sell it in many local farmers' markets.

What can we do?

Why not grow your own salad vegetables in the garden? By growing your own food, and buying less from the shops, you will help to cut down on food transport.

Farming begins at home

Large areas of forests are cut down to clear land on which crops can be grown for biofuels.

BETTER BUILDING

Better building makes for a better planet! Some homes and offices are built in places that destroy natural habitats.

What's the problem?

- Building materials, such as **concrete**, use up a lot of energy and water.

- Some builders use **hardwoods** from tropical forests. It takes a long time for the trees to grow again.

- We build homes on flat plains where rivers flood, which means the homes can also flood.

This farmhouse is surrounded by flood water.

What's the solution?

We should still build new homes. But we need to fill up all the empty houses first. We can build with **renewable** materials like straw bales.

What's going on near you?

Are there empty houses in your local area? How could the area be planned or built? Write your thoughts in a letter and send it to your local councillor.

ACTION AROUND THE WORLD

Nader Khalil is an architect who designs homes that are planet-friendly. He uses local materials such as clay and animal dung. These materials are perfect for his dome-shaped houses. These houses are built very quickly, too. This is why they have been used for homeless refugees. There are at least 500 million people without a home in the world today.

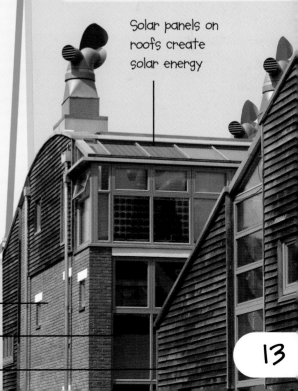

These BedZED houses in London, are a great example of housing that helps, not harms, the environment.

Solar panels on roofs create solar energy

30 cm (12 in) thick insulation on all walls

3 cm (1.2 in) thick triple glazing on windows

Local wood reduces transport pollution

FIGHTING THE FUMES

Take the bus, cycle, or walk to school and help stop global warming and climate change.

QUESTION BUSTING!

Q Aren't we all making a big fuss about burning fossil fuels?

A Absolutely not! Every year, about six billion tonnes of carbon fills the air. Every litre of petrol produces 2 kg (4.5 lbs) of **carbon dioxide**.

Q Diesel fuel is better than petrol, isn't it?

A Diesel engines burn about 30 per cent less fuel than petrol engines. So they make 30 per cent less carbon dioxide. But diesel engines release soot, which holds a lot of heat.

Q Are biofuels better than fossil fuels?

A Clearing land to grow cereals for biofuels is destroying the environment. However, by reusing cooking oil for biofuel, we can help the environment instead.

Action around the world

Cooking uses up a lot of fuel. In India, many people cook with biogas made from food waste or animal dung. The gases produced by burning biogas do not harm the planet. In richer parts of the world, cooking in a microwave can save about 70 per cent of energy.

What can we do?

Sharing a car journey to school can help save the planet. Car sharing saves fuel. It also saves time because fewer cars on the road reduce traffic.

Cycling is good exercise and helps save the planet.

Sharing a car journey can help save the planet

THINK ABOUT TOURISM

Hooray for holidays! Or is it? The planet isn't cheering. Long holiday journeys add to our carbon footprint. Many holiday resorts are spoiling natural environments. It's time to think about tourism.

THINK IT THROUGH!

One air journey can't hurt, can it? Well, it depends how far you go. If you fly from New York to London you help to pump out about 1.5 tonnes of carbon dioxide gas, as well as other harmful gases.

Airlines are using more planes and bigger planes to cope with all the holidaymakers. New runways and air terminals are spreading across the world. Building them uses precious energy.

Britons make 68 million trips abroad every year.

Action around the world

Tourism is good because it gives people jobs. But there is a flip side. The holidaymakers use up local water and energy and create a lot of waste.

You can go on holiday and help the planet. Some people go on holidays to clear up the countryside, trim hedges, mend fences, and clear ditches. This is called ecotourism, and it can be a lot of fun.

Beautiful coral reefs like these are damaged by sewage from hotels.

What can we do?

Make the most of where you live. Visit new places within walking distance or a short bus ride away. Find out about the history of your local area. Write down what you find out and draw some of the things you see. You could make a brochure for your local tourist office or library.

Make the most of where you live

Find out your local history

DRASTIC PLASTIC

From bags and bottles to wrapping and radios, plastic litter is everywhere. Plastic can be very useful, but it is polluting our planet.

Plastic hazards

Plastic can be bad news. It is made from petroleum, and smelly fumes fill the air when plastic is made. These fumes are bad for our health and can damage the **atmosphere**.

Plastic bottles take thousands of years to break up in landfill sites. Plastic bags choke birds, mammals, and sea creatures, and they block drains and cause floods.

Waste around the world

Every year, people throw away four billion plastic bags. Tied end to end, they would go around the Earth an amazing 63 times.

Many birds die each year because they eat rubbish such as plastic.

Save the Planet

Plastic litter is everywhere, so pick it up and try to reuse it.

* Show people just how many plastic bottles are thrown away each week by making a sculpture out of your household's bottles.

* Reuse plastic drinks bottles for your drinking water.

* REUSE plastic bags or just REFUSE them.

* Bangladesh has banned plastic bags. We could do it too!

Slick slogans

Slogans sell ideas. Think of some short, snappy slogans to point out the problems of plastic. You could try the slogans below and opposite.

Reduce, reuse, recycle!

"I am the problem. I am the solution."

SMALL STEPS, GIANT LEAPS

There are lots of things you can do to save our environment. You have read about some of them in this book. Every little change makes a big difference to our planet.

What's the problem?

The world is really warming up. Winters are milder, and spring flowers bloom earlier. The warm earth whips up stronger tornadoes, and warm seas contribute to devastating hurricanes. These things are happening in front of our eyes, so no one can deny that there is a problem. The next step is to do something about it.

Plant a tree! Trees will absorb harmful carbon gases.

What's the solution?

Let's reduce the amount of waste we produce. Reduce what we use, reuse what we have, and remember to recycle. We can do all these at home, at school, and on holiday. These small steps will help save energy and save the planet. It really is that easy.

LET'S BEGIN AT HOME!

Now that you have read this book, think about all the things you can do to make a difference. Write down a list. Here's a start:

* Take a shower instead of a bath.

* Turn the tap off when you clean your teeth.

* Use energy-saving light bulbs, such as the one shown in the picture opposite.

* Walk or cycle if you can.

* Reduce, reuse, recyle.

* Grow some herbs or vegetables.

You'll feel much better for it.
For you are helping to save our planet!

GLOSSARY

atmosphere the upper layer of gases around the Earth

bacteria tiny living cells. Some cause disease. Others clear up harmful waste.

biofuels fuels made from crops such as maize and palm oil

carbon dioxide a "greenhouse gas" released by burning fossil fuels. It helps form a layer of gases around the Earth that keeps in heat.

carbon footprint the amount of energy each of us uses

cereals foods from the seeds of grasses, such as wheat, maize, and millet

charcoal slowly-burned, charred wood. Charcoal is used for fuel and lasts longer than wood.

concrete a hard building material made by mixing cement, sand, gravel, and water

cosmetics creams, lotions, and make up used by people

fossil fuels fuels such as coal and oil, made from ancient plant and animal life

fungi a puffy growth a bit like a plant. Mushrooms are fungi.

habitats types of natural area, such as rainforests or grasslands

hardwoods slow-growing trees that take a long time to replace

livestock animals reared for food, such as cattle, goats, and sheep

mosses masses of tiny, plant-like leaves that make a soft, velvety covering

oxygen a gas that humans and creatures take in and use to keep their bodies working

recycling using something in a different way

renewable something that can be used over and over again

species types of plant or creature

timber trees cut down to make furniture, paper, and other products

FURTHER INFORMATION

Websites

Great "green" facts and projects including tree-planting campaigns at:
www.coolkidsforacoolclimate.com

You'll find tips on "go green", recycling, eco-travel, and food at:
www.ecofriendlykids.co.uk

On this United Nations website for the environment you'll find facts, competitions, and stories of young eco-warriors around the world at:
www.unep.org/Tunza

This gives lots of rainforest facts, games, and hot news:
www.kidssavingtherainforest.org/factsheet.php.htm

You will find loads of facts on energy sources and how they affect the environment at:
www.eia.doe.gov/kids

Books

Climate Change (Earth SOS). Franklin Watts (2008)

Recycle by Kay Barnham. Wayland (2008)

Save Water by Kay Barnham. Wayland (2008)

Waste and Recycling by Sally Hewitt. Franklin Watts (2008)

You Can Save the Planet by Rich Hough. A & C Black (2007)

INDEX